United States distributor

DUFOUR EDITIONS, INC.

Booksellers and Publishers

Chester Springs, Pennsylvania 19425

ANCHISES

also by C. H. Sisson

THE LONDON ZOO
NUMBERS
METAMORPHOSES
IN THE TROJAN DITCH
—Collected Poems & Selected Translations—

VERSIONS AND PERVERSIONS OF HEINE
CATULLUS
THE POETIC ART
—a Translation of Horace's *Ars Poetica*—
THE POEM ON NATURE
—a Translation of Lucretius: *De Rerum Natura*—

AN ASIATIC ROMANCE
—a Novel—
CHRISTOPHER HOMM
—a Novel—

ART AND ACTION
ENGLISH POETRY 1900-1950

THE SPIRIT OF BRITISH ADMINISTRATION
WALTER BAGEHOT

THE ENGLISH SERMON 1650-1750

C.H.SISSON

Anchises

poems

Carcanet New Press

Acknowledgements are due to the editors of the
following publications in which these poems have
appeared: *Agenda*, *Critical Quarterly*, *PEN New
Poetry* 1973/4 and 1975, *Poetry Dimension
Annual* 3 and 4, *Poetry Nation*, *PN Review*, *Poetry
Wales*, *Scotsman* and *The Times Literary Supplement*

SBN 85635 178 4

Copyright © C. H. Sisson 1976

First Published in 1976
by Carcanet New Press Limited
in association with Carcanet Press Limited
330-332 Corn Exchange Buildings
Manchester M4 3BG

Printed in Great Britain
by Eyre & Spottiswoode Limited
at Grosvenor Press, Portsmouth

CONTENTS

La vie est un sommeil: les vieillards
sont ceux dont le sommeil a été
plus long; ils ne commencent à se
réveiller que quand it faut mourir.

La Bruyère

SAINT-RÉMY

I should have descended, perhaps
The hill
On a May morning
Ma bello is it I can please you?
That can never be.
You have pleased, you have pleased, all the long living
Not a tear from me, I wipe it, in telling
Et les aïeuls, grandfathers, grandmothers,
Down the street, in procession.

Tears
Are not always there for the danger of having them
Sometimes they pour out
In pleasure over the thin cascade
Down the steps, from the sacred source
There is no pleasure like that of descending
Hand in hand, plucking the rosemary
Plucking the thyme.

Over this effete cavern the sun

Sets
Down the hillside, walking
Rosemary, this time
At the foot of the cavern where the nymph stood
I did not understand her, not I
The steps descend
There is an underworld, in that water

Black

I intend no evil, come a little nearer, plunge
The water is extremely salt, I did not
Expect this effect
Nor can understand it now.

Once below the stream, what pleasure
What shall be seen
Awash

I came back to the same shore
Wrapt in mist
Here I laid up my boat. It was
Centuries ago, the black prow
Still there in the sand
And the ghosts walking to and fro, my friends

Perhaps

However that may be there is no other
I would find myself beside
The light over these arenas is dead

It was a nice dream
But I do not know its meaning entirely
No truth that is understood is entire
For wondering I go
Into the crypt where St Martha
Obscured herself from me
Won't you lie under the apple tree
With Our Lady of the Pommiers?
No news is best news from those quarters
And yet silence
Cannot tell all there is to tell nor
Knowledge
Be without silence.

FRIGOLET

Thyme, and cicadas in the grass
The white light of idleness.
Empty as a shin-bone, a hare
Or a bird from anywhere

ALYSCAMPS

Old man of Alyscamps
Aren't they dead enough for you?
You, with your palsied pleasures,
Seeking marrow-bones among the dead?

COTIGNAC

River, deep as death, deeper, Avernus,
Red water of ox-hide, ox-blood, clouded,
Drawn across these caverns like a taut sheet,
What is down there, under the cliff edge,
Deeper than hell? Village
Lost to all time, under the sick archway,
The lost steps lead there, the life
Stirs like a movement of moss.

If I were to awake in that underworld, whom should I see?
Not Nestor, not Paris,
Not any heroic shadow, long putrescent,
Blown into dust: no woman
Caught my wandering eye last summer
Or any summer gone. The friends of shadows,
The commonplace merchants of ambition,
These are the ones, bragging in the market-place
So vain is all philosophy
My teeth were set on edge by such merchants
Half a caravan back: and when they came
To the high street where the palms set the form
It was eating and drinking who must,
Who laughed loudest, who spat,
While I stood by discreetly.
Worn hours! bitter heart! petty mind below all
No kiss of sun can cure, autumn eyes
Seeking rather between shadows the hurt.

There are gigantic shadows upon the cliff-face
I have seen them scowl and lour over the village.

All villages have them: they are the governors
Living among themselves without passions
Touching our parts. I had lived among them as evil
No man knew better their vain twists,
Admired what he hated most
Or so fell to dreaming of impossibles
Which are only eaten ambition
Knives in the heart, or pure reason.

A handful of almonds, a few grapes
All that the fine fingers could pick
Out of the residue of the world
Was not enough for this termagant.
The fine surface of bodies touched
By the sun and rendered potable
Was not enough for the eye-palimpsest;
The half-eaten moaner must moan.
What cages for tigers, whips for scorpions or other
Replicas of effete damnation
Had been prepared, must find a place
Within the cataclysm of each mind.
Mine was none of the stablest, I felt,
Looking over the impeccable scene,
The cicada chipping the hillside.

SILLANS-LA-CASCADE

Water falling over these rocks
Like tears
Not for myself, but for another.
Lovely hair, cascading over a brow
Troubled now. I saw her in sleep
So touching and so betrayed.
There is no enemy but the hater.
Once passed, once gone
There is no meeting but in Acheron
Where the full-fledged ghosts wait underneath
And the rock falls
Sisyphus.

What mind from under the dragon's tooth
Sprang in these places, tightened
Between rocks, fastening with chains
The innocent contender, the wise owl
Hoots from the barn.
It is morning under a steel sky,
The horses running;
A splinter of bones and a crucifixion
Against the sky.

Do not ask why I came to this place
To find
What I am better without,
Old memories, sudden as images
On the castle wall,
Armour and hard words.

This is the hour when my bones too
Are ground to powder;
The marrow snivels on to the path
And I am nowhere,
In the pool
Where the cascade falls and Acheron
Opens its gates.
I saw nothing of that in my book
But the mind
Returns to it and it does not leave me.

ENTRECASTEAUX

Entrecasteaux has hatreds
As other cities have loves
So had I but the teeth of the Sibyl

The juniper is bitter and the holm-oak is persistent
The juniper is masked and the holm-oak is hooded
Spring comes down the mountain

The juniper is abundant and the pine bobs before it
Atys your tree upon Mother Ida

Entrecasteaux has hatreds
As other cities have loves
So had I but the teeth of the Sibyl

Spring comes down the mountain to the narrow ravine
Twist your waters, avenging river

Entrecasteaux has houses
With rooms for intrigue and murder
But above all for persistent voices.

THE QUANTOCKS

Sheep under the beeches: the old dykes
Reflective over centuries, the sheep
Stationary over escaped time.
My nails are ground by biting,
There is no remembrance
Does not taste like aloes.

THE CLOUDS

Nothing, nothing came out of the dark evening.
First the river came, it was not in that.
Then I noticed the sun, falling over the hay-fields,
Behind mist—or cloud was it?—an obscurity—
Plunge westwards.

Fell evening, dragon, Tarasque,
Coming out of yourself, Phoenix,
Self-burning corn, smoke under your thatches:
No mean day must follow.

The nightingales are asleep.

GARDENING

What night, corrupt, as this must be, with dreams
Gathers around this age that finds me now
Here in this garden, not in Eden, no
Another garden and another time

But there is neither slope nor sun can make
Amends for what I missed under your hands.
Old fool. Reproaches I could buy for nothing
In any market-place. How can I turn
This ageing sorrow to a biting wind
To catch me like the tangles of your hair
Gone and imagined? Better than dreams
Is closing in the circle of the earth
Time out of mind.

SEED-TIME

Pinpoint seed or seedling I cannot tell which
So deep I look past the petalled leaves
Which once swayed for me as all
So deep
There can be no exchanges or crossed winds
Recognition is one-sided, I am invisible
Or should be, husk of myself.

So a bonfire burns and one looks into it
Fallen ash, green houses
Sticks
Charred till they whiten and the winking lights
Move round the bole.

There could be no meeting again on this earth
In any furrow or perhaps anywhere
Seed-time is a tear-drop carrying the eye
Into the interior of the womb, where hope lies
Crouched for its disappointment.

THE EVIDENCE

If you had hopes once they have turned to reason
If you had reason it has turned to evidence:
The evidence is against you.

PHILO THE MAGICIAN

They are going mad in there. His head was sloping
As he ran down the corridor
Square lights flashing, aluminium
A tinkle

There was murder done

The running man
Signified myself
But I, crossing cunningly from another direction
Collided with a grinning face, which is not mine ordinarily
But of which the yellow skull could be mine

'For thine is the kingdom'
Pulsated, I expect an orgasm
In the ugly night
Of the power and the glory
They passed like spectres beside my ear
Singing, pulsating
I do not want this dream and I do not want
Any

Who came, in this dream?
It was Philo the Almighty
Magician
Yet the face I saw?

It was like the nightingale
I remember now, in summer.

DIVINE POEMS

1

Work without hope is the best recipe
For a harmless life, if any life can be harmless
That is born of woman and goes back into the slot.
There was one, harmless, who came that way

2

A broken spirit, a contrite heart
Are acceptable, taken together
But the native spirit that I have broken
Does not go with contrition.

3

I can no more be contrite, God
Than I can understand your magnificence
A creeper here, a boaster there
My conscience is under the tarmac.

4

Abjection is also a vice
For there is nothing which could be abject
In nothing, which is what I am
Stamped with the maker's image.

EASTVILLE PARK

I sat on a bench in Eastville Park
It was Monday the 28th of October
I am your old intentions she said
And all your old intentions are over.

She stood beside me, I did not see her
Her shadow fell on Eastville Park
Not precise or shapely but spreading outwards
On the tatty grass of Eastville Park.

A swan might buckle its yellow beak
With the black of its eye and the black of its mouth
In a shepherd's crook, or the elms impend
Nothing of this could be said aloud.

I did not then sit on a bench
I was a shadow under a tree
I was a leaf the wind carried
Around the edge of the football game.

No need for any return for I find
Myself where I left myself—in the lurch
There are no trams but I remember them
Wherever I went I came here first.

MARCUS AURELIUS

I do not want to pour out my heart any more
Like a nightingale bursting or a tap dripping:
Father no more verses on me, Marcus Aurelius
I will be an emperor and think like you.

Quiet, dignified, stretched out under a clothes line
The garden of my soul is open for inspection
As the gardener left it, chaque cheveu à sa place
And if you do not believe me you can comb through my
      papers yourself.

Of course you may not agree with: No hurt because the
      lips are tight.
The psychologists have been too much for you, but that
      rascal Freud
Did nothing but devise his own superficial entanglements
For his readers to trip over, while he smiled.

Old devil of Vienna, moving among the porcelain,
You were the beetle under the ruins of an empire
And where the Habsburgs had protruded their lips
You pinched your nostrils.

If I were a plain man I would do the same,
Dexterous, money-making, conforming to another pattern
Than the one I seek which will cover me entirely:
I hope to be an emperor under my own mausoleum.

DROWNING

'With well-made songs, maintains th'alacrity
Of his free mind': or, as in my case, stutters
Eats out his heart at will, maintains friends
In expectation of loving, but does not love:
Twists words
Till they should have meaning, but they have none,
Kisses the earth, muddies his lips, and all this
Does not amount to a paid song, a footfall
Under the Almighty's feet, or a cool hand
Placed where I would place it, on the bare side
Of my shelled mistress, Anadyomene
Rising out of the sea in which I shall drown.

ONE EVENING

There are also bland days; they supervene
On fury and defeat
Open my side, see where the heart is

A smooth skin, traces of cool stone
But marvellous to the hand
What is there, Tertullian?

In my mind the roots quiver
Where will you touch, O root?
Mark this, the land set out.

But my mind is eaten by a strange fish
Chub or tench, stationary in the water
Only the lips moving.

IT IS

It is extraordinary how old age
Creeps on one
First it is not believed, even noticed
Then one notices symptoms but says nothing:
At the last nothing is what one says.

PERHAPS

Perhaps something was said
But now the man is dead
I cannot hear him now
I cannot hear him now
I cannot hear him now

Perhaps he spoke, but if he did
Nobody heard what he said
I cannot hear him now
I cannot hear him now
I cannot hear him now

Do not pretend to listen
It is of no importance
I cannot hear him now
I cannot hear him now
I cannot hear him now.

THE HOUSE

They went into the wall and became no one,
The best person to be, if you ask me
But their retreat could be painful to the bystanders
Who had seen them there and then again they were not,
Only the house with the clock ticking and the meals at
     regular intervals.
There are worse things than becoming a house.

THE GARDEN

Am I not fortunate in my garden?
When I awake in it the trees bow
Sensibly. There is a church tower in the distance,
There are two, underneath the maze of leaves

And at my back bells, over the stone wall
Fall tumbling on my head. Fortunate men
Love home, are not often abroad, sleep
Rather than wake and when they wake, rejoice.

ANTRES

Shade, shadow less than nothing within my dream,
Less than myself in that you have receded
Within this shell, yet more
In that you have gone further and fared worse, and also
    because
I pursue you still, and am unpursued
While it is I who am open to every persuasion

Yet within myself
There is no such thing as you are, I miss you
There are caverns you go through like an echoing voice
I am not even an echo
Yet all this is me, for it is not you

I cannot catch at my antres, or you wandering
Nothing therefore
And it is no use representing that as blackness,
Placing sentries, touching upon the walls
Though they drip moistly, suggesting downfall.

Nothing is not pepper or salt, or any taste
Cinnamon, ginger
It does not water the palate nor arrose the smell
Can it imagine, holding within itself
The recession of anybody?

THE CORRIDOR

1
Nothing is what I have done
Where I have been
These long years

No such thing
As metaphysical
Escape
There is a safe
Kind of body begins
With the toe
Continuing through
The bones of the foot:
Must I go
Through every damned bone,
Filament, ligament?

2
Yes, a figure like a light at the end of a corridor
Justice heard her voice
And with attention
Scored
Marks on the brightness
The inexpugnable wall

It was Atalanta ran down
Either foot equal, the hands
Flying like butterflies

3
It is not where I want to go
But I have no choice
Past the buildings, along the straight road
My thoughts with me, I do not want to take them

I plod on
The internal way is best, I am concentrated.
Down on my head a lead weight

Under my feet
The pavement
Rising so hard that my feet are splayed.
Smiling from the side-walk is inappropriate
My intent is serious
A small liar
Heading for an immutable destiny
In whatever disguises
I change my suit several times as I walk

There are dragons at some of the cross-roads
Hedged by privet
Dusty and dull and the long red-brick avenue
Will they reach me in time?
There is hardly a fear, I am so protected
The collar of my rain-coat turned up
The walls of the street and of my eyes so firmly blinded.

You could be lost before day break, if it will
Where are the snares
With which you were threatened?
Where are the entanglements
To trammel your feet and make the way less easy?
The very simplicity is deceptive
It is achieved by the rejection of voice
Touch, smell, taste
No music or shape, that is the best way
Say some

A morass of feet
Mine moving the least certainly among them
There is no way to go on
Which foot is mine?
I can no longer tell, I go all ways
At least there is mire, I am in it, there are others
Is this a walk or a rout?

Where are they going? How many feet have they got?
Where is the rest of them, baulking giants
Without any theory to account for them?

I have my theory, which is just this
From here I set out to there I go.

4
If I opened my eyes, what should I see
Any of this?
A crucifixion, with the blood dripping upon me

Or hands down
Picking a flower
Or exacerbating a butterfly
Taking the wings off a beetle?

Glory to God, three figures
Graces perhaps

5
There is no news Homer among the
Rushes, useless to pry, looking
Here and there in case anywhere there should be
Satyrs, leprechauns there is no news
Homer there is no news. I once saw
Homer advancing and peeping into a dustbin

6
I wanted a way out
From this
Neither can I think
Of any
Except

The paradigm
Of the extended body
Lying in furze
Under the sedge
Or twisted
Under effete grasses, dead also

Surely it stirs
Its moment has not yet come

Yet it will
When

Headlong

Out of the earth
Rising like a jaguar springing

Yet it is not like that
Smooth
Foiled

7
What night
Are you bound for?
Is there any?

I cannot answer that question, I am
Not the man who answers

Who are you then?

Not the man who answers
Not? Not
Not for any man
I am not the man who answers any questions.

Do you ask?

I do not ask
I am not the man who asks

Not? Not

I am not the man who asks

Who are you then?
Not the man
Not the man
Not
Not
Not

8
There is a thread I cannot follow it

There is a way
There is no other
Through darkness

Walk then
Long
Through the corridor

That is not a light then, though it is supposed to be
A lake rather
A guttering candle lights up the surface of it

Black light

I have gone through the door

9
I understand oceans, which do not change
In volume and composition, or not very much
Yet the surface changes, following the day's weather
The depth marches up, the superficial element
Bobs underneath more or less

Movement of sea, volume of water
Moving up from the depths, while the surfaces
Fall, losing themselves
Fathoms
Below, but do not sleep there, turning silently
While the great fish swim through them
—There is no seaweed
Below a certain depth, but—
In palaces
Darkness
The outcome of which
Cannot be guessed.
If there were an encounter
Could it be otherwise than of shadows?

10

The darkening shades are the way I go
How could it be otherwise? I come from lugubrious waters
The hunt and prayer of our hearts

11

Dreams are of no value
They move intangibly
Not turning the wheels
Not moving the limbs
Causing no embrace

12

I walk splendidly, and indirectly
Looking where I am not going
Blowing against closed doors, looking into the open ones.
Monsieur est distrait? He is plain distracted
Old hat askew, travelling boots
Travelling nowhere, or the toes pointed
In the direction opposite to movement, or 30°
Or 37°, or 2.5° or some odd
Measure of distraction from reality.
Behind his spectacles the eyes
Entertain improbable speculations
Rolling, rolling
With little half-movements, aspersions
On this or that aspect of reality.
Why will your feet not take the floor
Those large hands
Close over something not the edge of a mirror?
Dreams are of little value
Old hat, perforated head,
Stuffed with dreams
If that were all

But the direction of movement, the skid and skad
Drawing a circle where there should be a square.
The way it is worth going
Is not an easy one, for intellectual persons
Such as I, nauseous perhaps
To the more intelligent.

27

Out from under the body politic
Walking in twilight, one after another
Yet a conversation
Hurts, it is a string tied round the body

13
Hanging on a tree in the Garden of Eden
Thirteen days and thirteen nights
Give me some drink: hand me a loaf of bread
Down from the tree, I come and get it myself

There are saws and maxims enough

Before I can sing
Anything that I will
There must first be the elision
Of the individual mind,
Closed like a crack of the earth
The earth itself
Is what I now sing, wish to

14
The backward road
Must be under the marshes
Glutinous, harsh
Darker than ever, resistant
Darker than ever, I would go that way but I cannot

It must be darkness, whether forward or backwards
The light has left me
There is not even a marsh taper, a flicker
A deception one moment believed, though the next
    doubted
There is not even the taste of death if I go forward
For death is endless
Tasteless, it is infinite
The great cloak
Waiting to be put on
And when I walk in it
I should struggle like a caught thing wanting to use the flesh

Convinced for all eternity that I have it
Torn and feathered like a spent bird
Neither believing
Against my unbelief, nor holding solidly
While these tatters, my flesh
Blow away like salt to the edges of the universe
Death is the only costume I put on
It does not disguise me now, it is my own
Sleep I hoped for
Pre-monitor of the resurrection, mother of language
Leaves me now
Yet there is nothing it leaves
Sleep is for flesh
Such as I used to imagine
Not stretched like mine to the edge of the universe
Compacted marvels
There could be speech with, which, where I now am, is not.
It is not silence, which I have also known, for that is the
    cessation
Of rustling. Where I am now
There are no leaves to stir or cease from stirring

Avert my eyes, I am no longer required
Where the dragons walk, there is certainty
Where the angels
Fling up their trumpets, there is mediocrity
Where peace is
There I would go forward, and not be I
The Incarnation
Came suddenly
In another place, and I no longer stand there

I am on the edge, beyond the touch of reason
As of the flesh
If a word takes me, it is in its flight
From another mouth
It cannot be my ear
Hears

15

The indisputable master of all this,
Old age
Assays no more the gold under his hand
The ways you did not follow matter more
Than those you did
That is why eyes look past
The things you love to those you did not love
The hand is cupped
To catch the silence as it falls between
The chatter that you did not want to hear:
The man who would be off is dead already.

THE LIZARD

Plant thrift and do not marry
Samphire and throw yourself over a cliff.

ANCHISES

This is my proper order: sightlessness,
The invisible pack hunting the visible air.
There are those who exist, but it is not I.
Existent are: bodies, although their existence is
Not proven; tremors
Through the vast air expecting some other thing
Not known, or hopeless; or else hoped for and lost.
One could devise invisibility,
Walking by it as if it were not obligatory
As it is with me, *moi qui n'existe pas*
NON SUM, therefore NON COGITO, although there are
        shapes
Upon a mind I sometimes take to be mine.
This is not much to show for sixty years
Here by the Latin gate, or where the Baltic
Spreads its white arms over the barren sand.

Do not number me on this seashore
Where the effete light from the north
Floods over the ice-cap. I came from Troy
It was not after she had ended, but before.

OVER THE WALL: *Berlin, May 1975*

1

He will go over and tell the king
Or whoever is top dog in that country
How there is feasting here, the wastes are empty
The nine governors sleeping

Not a prophetic sleep, with the lids opening
Upon passion, dreaming of conflict
But the eyes turned inwards so that the whites
Gaze upon the world, and the heart ticks steadily
To the combustion of a strange engine
Not in the heart, more like a bee
Buzzing in the neighbourhood. Lost heart, lost head
There is no reflection under the cool brain
Which thinks only of last night's dominoes,
Glibly at least. Over the wall,
Knives drawn, teeth drawn back,
Swallowing the rattle they make in case the night
Should interpret their wishes.
Here in the west, far west, slumber
While death collects his paces.

I am not warlike but, once the frontiers are falling
Each man must put on his belt, it has been done before
And the whimpering must stop, Death being the kingdom
Of this world.

2

I have seen the doomed city, it was not my own
Love has no city like this, with barred hatreds
All bitterness, all shames. I do not think there is any

31

Feast to be eaten or long shawls
Trailed in the dust before the fanatic mob
Only quiet people live here, eating their sandwiches
Under the lilac while the boats go by,
Interminable imitation of reality
Which is not to be had, and should the frost fall
Should the eagle turn its head
The city of too many desperate adventures
I have seen them all, or so it seems, the Uhlans . . .
And now from the steppes
It is as if the Dalmatian horsemen came back,
Yet they do not stir, or make themselves visible . . .
One street I remember
There is no majesty in its lost endeavours
Speak to me no more, I have heard only
The marching men.
Sleep comes to those who deserve
Funerals under the chipped archways.

3
I do not think this is the end of the story
There are battalions enough behind the wall.
The tall policemen bent over me like the priest
Of an evil religion, as if I were the elements
And he the emissary who was empowered to transform me.
That was not the same
Dream-ridden solitude I had known before
Where a flame climbed the walls there was no one by.

4
I know only aspen, beech, oak
But here on these wastes the turtle
Sang among the sands, sitting upon a pine-tree
No man has meditated this regress
Yet the afternoon sun falls upon faces
Less tame than tigers.

LANGPORT

The elder tree grows by the rhine
White elder, red elder
The elder tree grows by the rhine
Black elder, oh!
I walked this way in a shower of rain
Nothing is dry when I walk here again
Tears drenched my eyes oh!
Ham-stone fritters and gables of play
The sun is out with the moon today
Ten fine muskets out in a line
Nine of them twisted down in the rhine
Ten twisted elbows there in the rhine
Ten wrenched shoulders there in the rhine
Ten humped bodies down in the rhine
Red elder oh! black elder oh! white elder!

AN ELM WITHERED
BY THE DUTCH ELM DISEASE

A score of rooks on a withered tree
What news from Barbary?
A score of rooks on a withered tree
Tartary hordes oh!
Look, is that a man in the hedge?
Is that a rifle? Who are the others?
They cannot all have come down from the hill.
Or did they? And why? Will they scare the rooks?
They come too quietly. Why do they stand?
They have advanced to the edge of the land
They are walking now: and the heron will rise
And the rooks will clamour against the skies.
There will be shots, but the bastinado
Is not intended to beat up the partridge.
Trees wither oh! elms wither oh!
Trees wither!

33

THE NOYADE

This is not a satire, nor indeed an invention of any kind. The Fifth Edition of the Dictionnaire de l'Académie Française, *published in 1813, has a supplement containing the new words which had come into use since the Revolution, with new senses for some old words.*

The vocabulary of the Revolution, it seems,
Was much the same as the one we use at present,
    Which shows that in liberating the human spirit
    The *grands ancêtres* provided amusement for centuries.

Administration centrale is one of these,
As also the *administrations intermédiaires*
    With the *administrateurs* and the *adjoints*
    Engaged in the new administrative employments.

A also contains the useful word *amendement*
In the sense of a 'modification proposed to a draft
    Of a law or decree to render it more precise';
    Why else should anyone propose an amendment?

There is also *anglomane* and *anglomanie*,
Which sound odd now, but England was then the exemplar
    Of an imaginary liberty which attracted the writers
    Who, then as now, wrote faster than they understood.

Aristocrate—it was nothing to do with aristocracy;
But 'the name given to the partisans of the old régime'
    —A kind of lying which has been improved on since:
    Think a moment and you will remember our words.

In A I might also mention *arrestation*,
'The act of arresting a person', much practised by citizens
    Who regarded the appellation 'subject' as odious
    And declined to pronounce it, in their political chatter.

B was for *barrières* 'placed upon the frontiers,
With offices designed for the collection of taxes'
    Though one knows that, in fact, the barriers had other
        uses:
    There was no more going abroad without a passport.

Bureau central, bureaucratie, bureaucratique
Place, function and qualification are now universal;
    It was, after all, for mankind in its generality
    That the Revolution was made, not for those who
        inhabited

A mere particular village, town, city or country.
C: and observe the history of *carmagnole*,
    'The name at first of a dance, and then a shirt,
    Afterwards of the soldiers who wore that uniform':

Finally—because a soldier is only a soldier
When he is used by somebody, *carmagnole* achieved a
        new dignity
    As 'the designation of a certain kind of report
    Treasured in the bosom of the National Assembly'.

I say nothing of *centimètre* and *centralisation*,
Citoyen, civisme—'the zeal which inspires the citizen'—
    Or *carte de sûreté*—something for paid-up members—
    Or *club, conscrit,* or *conscription militaire.*

O Liberation! those were inventive days.
Contre-révolution—but better have nothing to do with it.
    Démocrate, démocratie—'is employed at present
    In the sense of attachment to the popular cause'.

Département, for an administrative area
Bearing no relation to the place people live in;
    Déporter, 'a revival of the old Roman banishment'
    —You were lucky if you got out: *détention*,
    imprisonment.

I pass over E—though it covers new kinds of *écoles*—
To arrive at F, and the *fonctionnaire public*;
   Fournée, once the word for a batch of loaves,
   Becomes a cartload of people condemned to the
      guillotine.

G is for *garnisaire*, 'a man put in garrison
With taxpayers who have got behind with their taxes';
   Grand-juge-militaire, 'in each arrondissement';
   Also for *guillotine*, 'perfected by a doctor

To cut off heads by a mechanical operation'.
Homme de loi—H—is the name given to the *légiste*
   'Instructed in the most modern jurisprudence'.
   Indemnité, 'the pay of members of parliament'.

I pass over K, for *kilolitres* of blood,
To get to L, for hanging on lamp-posts or *lanternes*
   —Which explains how *liberté* acquired its new meaning
   Of 'doing whatever does no harm to others'.

M, the *majorité*, still of major importance;
Maison d'arrêt, a place of arrest or *détention*;
   Masse, 'collectively, all together, especially
   To go *en masse*, with the crowd, as in an assembly'.

Neutralisation—of treaties, so 'only provisional'
—Unlike the fate of those who suffer in *noyades*,
   Which is pushing a boatload of unpopular people
   To the middle of a river, after making suitable plug-holes.

O, *organiser*, in the sense of 'organising
All the interior movements of any body';
   Passer à l'ordre du jour, as in an assembly,
   To avoid the discussion of anything too awkward.

P is the *Panthéon français*, designed for the cinders
Of those who are favourable to the Revolution;
   Permanence, in the sense that a public assembly
   May be *en permanence*, and never stop talking.

Préhension, for the seizing of any commodity
Which has been made the subject of price regulation;
    And *propagande, propagandiste*, a body or person
    Charged to promote the most acceptable principles.

Q—a *Quiétiste*, used to designate persons
Who do not join in the fun of the Revolution;
    And a *question préalable* is simply the Question
    Of whether a Question had better not be discussed.

For R we have *radiation*, the rubbing out
Of the names of people you are advised to think no
      more of;
    Réfractaire, for those who have proved refractory
    And therefore must be excluded from their functions.

Réquisition, 'not only used of commodities
But of young men who are needed for military service'.
    S for *septembrisade*, a general massacre,
    And the verb *septembriser*—'she was septembred'.

Souverain—'the universal collection of citizens'
—Except the *suspects*, suspected of being indifferent;
    Which brings us to T and to Terror,
    Terroriste, terrorisme, in the end thought slightly
      excessive.

Travailler is working, but not in the sense of producing
Anything more substantial than disaffection
    'In favour of a faction'; and T is also *tyrannicide*
    —Only be careful that you name the right tyrant.

The alphabet is exhausted with U and V;
Urgence, 'the pressing need for a resolution',
    —A *résolution urgente*, there are no others.
    V, *vandalisme*, 'destroying the arts and sciences'.

V has a final fling with *vocifération*,
'A clamorous way of proceeding in assemblies';
    And *visites domiciliaires*—you can guess who visits.
    The man they are looking for might have written this.

SWIMMING THE HORSES
To Pippa and David

Swimming the horses at Appleby in Westmorland
—Or Cumbria as they now call it, God damn their eyes.
The rest of the verses *desunt*: they were meant to say
Damn all politicians and bureaucrats
Who cannot make fires with uncertain materials.
They imagine that their voices will be heard above
The ripple of rivers and the song of cuckoos—
Which they will not be, or not for long
If they continue with their inordinate charges
To feed reputatious mouths, or none at all
And think that generations of mud-eaters
Can be stamped out to serve a committee slicker
—As they can indeed, but eaten by a dust
That will soon settle over the whole of England.
Those who kick their ancestors in the teeth
Prosper for a time, but in adversity,
Which soon comes, there is a change.

THE SPIDER

Carry, tarantula, into your house in the shade
This iota of meaning: that man's dream
Fled as I twanged the wire and let him go
It is with me he would have disappeared.

DROUGHT

The sun has risen over the parched plain
Where the water was, gold drops
Fall, thicker than hay-seeds through the light
Golden the floor on which the light pours
Golden the sky beyond the dark hills.
The Golden Age has come back, with metallic hand
To touch the drought, and spring is senile.

THE END

I shall never hear the angelic choir
Sing, as it assuredly does, I shall walk in hell
Among tinkers and tailors and other riff-raff.
Another damnation for imagining myself among those
Whose fornications came as easy as winking
And whose pilferings of other people
Were a social bounty which did not stop at themselves.
I knew early what there was to be known about me
Only lacked courage, fortitude, *élan*
And so descended into a consuming whirlpool
Round and round, here I am at the last gurgle.

VIRTUE

Virtue instead of failure, a fine choice,
Virtue is its own damnation. I, who see man
In his external shape, acting and bowing,
Take no account of his inner movements
Which are lies only, must admit
Myself virtuous although my heart is a sink
Where ambition swills round with lost lust
And even the last words are spoken with envy.

SUNSHINE AND RAIN

Each day is so brief, a tiny spasm
Of light between dark. It is falling now
Having shone brightly between darks.
How is it? Once the days were long
Nights were unseen, unless in a flash of terror.
But all is night now, where I move
What I taste smells of dark. To my lips I take
A mushroom falling to powder, an orange agaric
Unnatural as nature has now become
Shining there in the dark, between sunshine and rain.

THE WEATHER

The weather is most noticeable, for what else
Should I notice, I who have become wropped
In my own silence, no word saying anything
Although I speak it? Others' words come gently,
Like breezes, they are of uncertain origin
They come round a bush with surprise, through the
    willows,
A heron carries them. If there were any speech
It would be of roses, blackberries trailing
Over the effete comfrey. Spoiled is the world
Spoiled, autumn says, and so say I.
Neat words then, better than none at all,
Talking of nothing while night falls.

THE INSCRIPTION

It says that my work is done. Why do I wait
Here on this threshold?

Are there any more words to say? I do not think so.
Those I had did not reach the things I had.
Now on this threshold where I wait for death
To invite me in, I cannot remember my needs.
There are no beggars now, it is absurd for an old man
To stand suppliant even before his memories.
Why imagine what you cannot encompass?
It was not my need, I have none
But the supposed voice of the incorrigible Adam
Who knew Lilith in deep sterility and begot on Eve
Pro-figures of his departed desires
On which the world was built. It bursts out
In thunder and lightning in the following of Adam
And still lours over the horizon. I am not flesh
More than in his dream, the following of Adam
Enacting perilously before my eyes
What I have a part in, though I stand from it

Distant, above two hundred paces, a spectator,
Seeing what I am not and cannot touch,
Being what I want and cannot be.
O gateway! Downwards, I pour myself a libation
Dis manibus.

It is a rich country and I am in it. Every rat
Peeps from his cellar, every cat extends
His flattened body under the hoisted fur.
Leave me alone in this street. The houses topple

It broke through. It was not death that it came to.
Death is the surrounding country. In this city
Other manners prevail.

                        Who are they, my comrades?
Alive or dead, whatever I am myself.

This city I revisited on a day
The ghosts were paler, I had seen them all before
But less perfect, their eyes less direct. It was evening
Before, with the dusk hiding them, now it was morning.
Each face shone in its light, waxy, corrected,
Hair parted more than normally straight.
What eyes were those? The eyes of the dead or the living?
Did they see? If so, was it me they saw?
Why look past me as if I were not there?
Were they looking at anything? Could they see one
        another?
It is a strange city which has no citizens
And yet it seemed that these did not belong
I saw no couple clutching, heard no timbre
Of affection in any voice. There were no words,
At least they had not the intonation of language.
There are three numbers which, if I can remember them
Seemed significant. There was a prize Almighty
Sitting at the end of the street like a statue of Baal,
Hooting through the wind-pipes. Perhaps this was the one
Behind whom struggle the still sensible dead
Like a basket of serpents. Down the street came marching

Four-square, evocative, echoing, like armed soldiers
The damned dreamers exercised without sexes.
Huzzas from the windows, but the spectators listless.

I stopped by the bridge and watched the procession pass
They walked into the air or out of the gate:
I was for a darker dream. Under the river
Into which he fell, through the surface, black sinews
Closing over his head.

               Not formed
Nothing but darkness, the hell
Of a lack of expectancy, the river
Itself gone, not even an underground flow,
Nothing from a to b, no a or b,
No confinement or even location.

ULYSSES

Ulysses in your boat
In the curved waters where the eddies are
As the stream turns

                an old dressing-gown
Swirling in the water
           round and round
Where is Sackcloth?
            drowned drowned drowned.
Out from the river-mouth
          into the sea
Ulysses, traveller, glides on top

Out on the incalculable sea, new stories
Ringing in his ears, he has made them up,
Towards the Pillars
Standing at the edge of the desolate sea
Or so they think
Edges beyond edges

What fell
Over the bridge, into the river, is here before them
A ghost
Laughing in the mists beyond the Pillars of Hercules
(I have no desire to continue this)
Beyond the Pillars

I want to know which way they went
Which way they were delivered
One pole toppled over, the sky
Full of stars, showering the boat fore.
Aft, like a wake, the bubbles receded
That sky dying out

Having departed from Circe
In a small boat with a few educated companions
Who understood that subtraction
And did not want mercy, they were too advanced for it

Peace now, under the wind
Under the keel the barnacle
Considers

Baffled like a ghost tied to the mast, unwillingly
I went from Circe
Torn by the wind, fastened by recollection
Over the peak
Of one wave falling into the trough of another
I had come over vast times as well as waters
Africa on one side, Spain on the other
I do not remember when I drifted through
Into the Atlantic drain

It does not matter how the dice fall, here on shipboard
She runs south homing on the mountain of purgatory.
It is the whirlpool. The wind came from the mountain
Like a whiplash. The boat gurgled and fell

A curl of smoke
Rose from the conical mountain against a blue
Paler than light.

SEA-FALL

Amiable world
Why have you been so little to my liking?

No touch is best
No horror

                        Against the world
I had taken arms, and lost. They were not the arms
Of charity, than which there are no others
Prevail. I stumbled, walked and stumbled
And now I am sorry for what I did not do

Now if I am the enemy of myself
It is because love failed, my own.
Temper the wind to the giants, the performers
Have more need perhaps. Yet I
Am only need. It is myself
Which I have denied, and should, yet
Without whom, what am I? Nothing.

Tolerate nothing, it is extravagant
To hope. So the wind changes
Nor' nor' east, nor' nor' west.
Gone
Over the headland the gull
Drifts

Wind, water, cliff, the last sight of
Land.

THE TURN-DOWN

1
It is idiotic to pretend to
Any particular knowledge of anything,
As, the making of soup, writing of poems,

Things which succeed sometimes, and sometimes not.
Any certainty in the matter of future
Or even past events, is an imbecility
—Not exactly that, for the imbecile moment
Is that of retraction from a single hypothesis
In order to take up position with another,
Or that of the return journey which will probably hit
Not the setting-out point but another mark,
A mad pendulum swaying, not to and fro
But this way and that, sideways, all ways.
There is no position which can be called Is,
The best names, therefore, are those which assert nothing,
Not, as abstractions do, comport a theory.
So the names of objects, stone, tree-trunk, branch,
Sky if you will, cloud, go far enough.

2
Action is not always murder, though murder
Is the fruit of action, the sequelae
In more or less, of the once decided
Apposition of cheek to wind or resolution to
    independence,
A dangerous, however small, movement of the mind
Towards the non-acceptance of what is acceptable.
No resolution is best, it is not needed
Where the balance is perfect, the rays fall
Equally.

3
I did not have what I wanted, when I wanted it
And now what I want is to want nothing more,
A form of death, but not a super-abundance.
Holà there servants, bring me a pot of nothing,
Extinction is in the cup, and I will drain it.

4
No further from, or to, is the plain decision
Of the do-nothing, say-nothing, waiting for everything
—The last thing that is likely to appear, if you ask me
But even you would be wiser than to do that.

5
Nothing to look back on, for everything has succeeded
A miracle, with the exception of myself.
That is to say each thing has been played out
To its bitterest end, nothing is left unfinished
To be regretted, continued or re-commenced.

THE WELL

Grave speech, but it is not my will
Not my words, as I speak them ordinarily
The speech that I wanted is not the speech that I have

Who spoke it? I
Waited by the side of a well
Not for any master, not for a frog to jump
It was mere distraction. The good names,
When they come, come softly. Charity
Is not in my heart, nor love
Even of spiders. There is no miraculous intrusion
No sound of voices, only the pen automatically
Doing what the body tells it, the silent one
Who never spoke by any issue of consciousness
Nor can plan its actions

There are many lives but only one dream
To which does the body belong? The many lives
I alone have lived, and do live, simultaneously
Not living but acting, being them without consciousness.
Can a voice come from that? Or from the dream,
Somatic perhaps, which the iron touches now
There are more kings than emperors, we
Are numerous enough, who are neither. The twitching
    hand,
Twitching mind may be subject, yes
Where it is to be read and
Silence becomes shapes.

SIMOIS

Well I remember that dark night in Troy
To whom was the moon friendly?

The Simois flows
Into the green

It is another world, thin
As paper
Cattle
Painted upon it, horses
Raising themselves

I want only to die
No other
Stands over against me now

Caught in the same vice
Screwed
Under the same press

One turn more
Of the great wooden handle and the thread
Bites deeper

Subject not object
And therefore bodiless
As leaf, crown, cattle are

Damned leaf
Hanging on the last tree in hell
My only love.

THE FIRE-BIRD

1
O darling Lesbia
What word can I write for you?
This is not a poem
It is not the digested
Matter of a thousand days
But the growth of one
Rising like a miraculous
Plant and bearing its leaves
Unsteadily in the air

And then your voice
And those hands
Fingers between my own
That brow
Bent half upon me, but half away
O other half
Come to me. Be me
In replacement of this
Tatterdemalion
Shadow I am.

2
So long matured
This wish
Born before you, with you and after you
And now here
This miraculous presence
Cannot be counted in days
There are no hours

Because I imagined you
Before you came
Yet did not imagine your hair
Your eyes
Did not imagine how you would be, or why
Where you would come from
Only
That you might

It is an extraordinary fortune
Which has brought you at last
I do not thank you
Only take you

3
It happened before time
Which is old already
Though not in you

It happened before touch
Look, or imagination
There were no eyes in it

But now that the eyes play
On what was not imagined
Could not be
Was not

4
What will be the answer?
You must say.
You are not allowed
To hinder or prevent
What was settled before
You had any reason
Settled when I was
In spite of your years
Which are none

5
Useless to run
Where you are, I am
Useless to stay still
You will melt in my arms

6
There must be no turning back
This is the way, we must go there
It will not be easy, all things are difficult, but
Confusion if we do not go

So I have clarified my mind, do you likewise
You are intellectually precise, it is your duty
Precision does not end with two words it is
The continuing victory of its own effort
—Not so much effort—
Has to be lived out, like poetry, to the end of the line
Not chosen exactly, delivered and not prohibited
That is all you can say
It is this precision
Leads to your bed, or to my rejection

7
But do not be in love oh not in love
That is what we cannot help it is not our doing
It is the choice which determines the love, there is only a
    choice
Of whether this must be, but not of me

8
I am burning to death and you let me
Fire-bird, for you are burning in my flame

TROIA

So in the morning light she came to him
Light-footed

But Troy the common grave of Europe and Asia
Troia (nefas)

The Sibyl's cave
Aeneas standing there
and it was only a descent

ad inferos
Speaking any words
wildly
Hair streaming: Aeneas founding a city
among the dead

Troy speaking again
only through the mouths of the dead
the city pardoned
the libation poured out and the ox-hides spread

I noticed this peculiarity in Troy
That the soldiers, looking out over the walls
Were sightless, they had long been dead
and a Roman capital
Stood in the desert, half broken.

THE DEW

Ros, ros
roris, the dew
'raus, heraus
Speaking no words, retreating
with a gun pointing at him

the frame of the door

backwards

But Ow!
a hand seized his hand
behind his back
'Down on your face
Eat the dust, eat the dust
Sir
Down on your face!'

A jackboot on your neck
a boot advances
also from the front
to push your skull in

These were the habits among which I was brought up
And I fear not altered.

CATO

How can I climb the Mount of Purgatory?
Cato, are you there?
—Looking so virtuous while your dream associates,
Dante and Virgil, cough behind their hands.

I who have never seen the last evening
—No more had Dante then—slip in behind
It is not for me to intrude upon the company
No supreme lady called me; if I go upwards
It will be stumbling, by myself, unobserved.
I should avoid all company on the way
And fall flat on my face if I saw Paradise,
Over the loose screes till I hit the earth
Head-first. There is so little content in this idea
Of a progression towards beatitude.
Beatitude is here or not at all
'The kingdom of heaven is at hand', or under the counter
For special purchasers who have enough money,
Coin of Caesarea. I wanted three things,
Lechery, success, never at any time virtue
But a faint approbation that makes life tolerable
As long as one lives in the city of weak smiles.
I have run counter to every device
That could bring happiness as I suppose it
Which is quite contrary to the way I have it.
O my dear absent one, oh my dear absence
When shall I be absent from myself?
Absence is mourning; absence is also love;
That presence may be love is all I pray.
I wait here and hope it may be morning.

THE QUESTION

Questi non vide mai l'ultima sera

1

No praise for anything but love
The body rhymes with helpless times
No praise for anything but love.

How often, Sibyl, have I wept
To touch the body as I would
How often, Sibyl, have I wept

My mind is now the only space
In which your body is at ease
My mind is now the only space

My word is now the only hand
That touches you, that touches you
My word is now the only hand

Your lips are now the only lips
To speak the words that I would speak
And I am not the man to hear

2

No speech in summer. Now the light
Falls upon apple-flower and blue-bell
You are not here. No more am I.

The water rushing past my ears
I stood there. You had gone away.
Now you were here. Now gone away

You waved across the standing car
Useless to turn the mind away
It homes upon you like a bolt.

3

What I felt when your post-card came.
I had retracted every wish
For every wish I had is vain.

Turn mind, like Whittington. I turn, I spin
Nowhere is London. Like a heap of sticks
I burn and crackle till I fall to ash.

4
One word would be enough. Better, a kiss
And best a night of love with my fell hand
Racing your belly while I kept your eyes.

Harsh senile dreams. I spit them from my mind
And have no peace until I stamp you out.
Or ever? Not because of you, my dear

Nor anyone. Because a bitter mind
At sixty years can have no peace at all

5
So turn to God. The old immutable
Accessible great mountain of my soul.
Here on the lower slopes I will remain.

No mind can master me. I pick no flower
But kick and scuff the pebbles in the stream.

EST IN CONSPECTU TENEDOS

1
The day goes slowly, it is the first day
After the fall of Troy. I walk upon the beaches,
A ghost among ghosts, but the most shadowy I
O Tenedos O the thin island
Hiding the ships. They need not hide from me
I am the least figure upon the shore,
Which the wind does not notice, the water refract, or the
    sands count
As one of their number. I was a warrior,
Yes, in Troy
Before all reason was lost.

Where did Helen come from? Where is she now?
All reason is lost and so is she.
I was only a parcel of her reason
Now of her loss
Ghosts
Cannot be companionable; parts, shreds,
All that I am, ghost of a part of a part

2
Desolate shore, dark night
I have lost so much that I am not now myself
That lost it, I am the broken wind
The lost eagle flying, the dawn
Rising over Tenedos

3
Not any more I, that is the last thing
Rise or fall, sunrise or sunset
It is all one. The moon is not friendly
No, nor the sun
Nor darkness, nor
Even the bands of maidens bringing offerings
Pouring libations, buried
Among the ineluctable dead.

4
Dead, ineluctable, certain
The fate of all men.